This Aircraft
Spotting Book
Belongs to

_____
_____
_____
_____

Aircraft Name_____

Aircraft Dimensions
Overall Length:

Height:

Fuselage Diameter:

Wingspan:

Wing Area:

Design Weight

Maximum Take Off Weight

Maximum Landing Weight

Launched in:_____ Based on:_____
First Flight: _____ Entry Into Service: _____

————— Basic Operation Data —————

Engine Information:_____
_____

Transport Capacity:_____
_____

Range: _____
_____

————— Aircraft Spotted —————

Date/Time Spotted _____

Where/Location   _____

Airport Details   _____

Notes
_____
_____
_____
_____

Aircraft Name _____

Aircraft Dimensions
Overall **Length:**

Height:

Fuselage Diameter:

Wingspan:

Wing Area:

Design Weight

Maximum Take Off Weight

Maximum Landing Weight

Launched in: _____ Based on: _____
First Flight: _____ Entry Into Service: _____

———————— Basic Operation Data ————————

Engine Information: _____
_____

Transport Capacity: _____
_____

Range: _____
_____

———————— Aircraft Spotted ————————

Date/Time Spotted _____

Where/Location _____

Airport Details _____

_____

Notes
_____
_____
_____
_____

Aircraft Name _____

Aircraft Dimensions
Overall Length:

Height:

Fuselage Diameter:

Wingspan:

Wing Area:

Design Weight

Maximum Take Off Weight

Maximum Landing Weight

Launched in: _____ Based on: _____
First Flight: _____ Entry Into Service: _____

——————— Basic Operation Data ———————
Engine Information: _____

_____

Transport Capacity: _____

_____

Range: _____

_____

——————— Aircraft Spotted ———————
Date/Time Spotted _____

Where/Location _____

Airport Details _____

_____
Notes
_____
_____
_____
_____

Aircraft Name _____

Aircraft Dimensions

Overall **Length:**

Height:

Fuselage Diameter:

Wingspan:

Wing Area:

Design Weight

Maximum Take Off Weight

Maximum Landing Weight

Launched in: _____ Based on: _____
First Flight: _____ Entry Into Service: _____

———— Basic Operation Data ————

Engine Information: _____
_____

Transport Capacity: _____
_____

Range: _____
_____

———— Aircraft Spotted ————

Date/Time Spotted _____

Where/Location   _____

Airport Details   _____
_____

Notes
_____
_____
_____
_____

Aircraft Name _____

Aircraft Dimensions

Overall Length:

Height:

Fuselage Diameter:

Wingspan:

Wing Area:

Design Weight

Maximum Take Off Weight

Maximum Landing Weight

Launched in: _____ Based on: _____
First Flight: _____ Entry Into Service: _____

———— Basic Operation Data ————

Engine Information: _____

_____

Transport Capacity: _____

_____

Range: _____

_____

———— Aircraft Spotted ————

Date/Time Spotted _____

Where/Location _____

Airport Details _____

Notes

_____
_____
_____
_____

Aircraft Name _____

Aircraft Dimensions
Overall **Length:**

Height:

Fuselage Diameter:

Wingspan:

Wing Area:

Design Weight

Maximum Take Off Weight

Maximum Landing Weight

Launched in:_____ Based on:_____
First Flight: _____ Entry Into Service: _____

———— Basic Operation Data ————
Engine Information:_____
_____

Transport Capacity:_____
_____

Range: _____
_____

———— Aircraft Spotted ————
Date/Time Spotted _____

Where/Location   _____

Airport Details   _____
_____

Notes
_____
_____
_____
_____

Aircraft Name_____

Aircraft Dimensions

Overall Length:

Height:

Fuselage Diameter:

Wingspan:

Wing Area:

Design Weight

Maximum Take Off Weight

Maximum Landing Weight

Launched in:_____ Based on:_____
First Flight: _____ Entry Into Service: _____

———Basic Operation Data———

Engine Information:_____
_____

Transport Capacity:_____
_____

Range: _____
_____

———— Aircraft Spotted ————

Date/Time Spotted_____

Where/Location   _____

Airport Details   _____

Notes
_____
_____
_____
_____

Aircraft Name _____

Aircraft Dimensions
Overall Length:

Height:

Fuselage Diameter:

Wingspan:

Wing Area:

Design Weight

Maximum Take Off Weight

Maximum Landing Weight

Launched in:_____ Based on:_____
First Flight: _____ Entry Into Service: _____

———— Basic Operation Data ————

Engine Information:_____
_____

Transport Capacity:_____
_____

Range: _____
_____

———— Aircraft Spotted ————

Date/Time Spotted _____

Where/Location   _____

Airport Details   _____
_____

Notes
_____
_____
_____
_____

Aircraft Name _____

Aircraft Dimensions
Overall Length:

Height:

Fuselage Diameter:

Wingspan:

Wing Area:

Design Weight

Maximum Take Off Weight

Maximum Landing Weight

Launched in: _____ Based on: _____
First Flight: _____ Entry Into Service: _____

———— Basic Operation Data ————

Engine Information: _____
_____

Transport Capacity: _____
_____

Range: _____
_____

———— Aircraft Spotted ————

Date/Time Spotted _____

Where/Location   _____

Airport Details   _____

_____

Notes
_____
_____
_____
_____

Aircraft Name _____

Aircraft Dimensions
Overall **Length**:

Height:

Fuselage Diameter:

Wingspan:

Wing Area:

Design Weight

Maximum Take Off Weight

Maximum Landing Weight

Launched in:_____ Based on:_____
First Flight: _____ Entry Into Service: _____

———————Basic Operation Data———————
Engine Information:_____
_____

Transport Capacity:_____
_____

Range: _____
_____

————————— Aircraft Spotted —————————
Date/Time Spotted _____

Where/Location   _____

Airport Details   _____
_____

Notes
_____
_____
_____
_____

Aircraft Name_____

Aircraft Dimensions

Overall Length:

Height:

Fuselage Diameter:

Wingspan:

Wing Area:

Design Weight

Maximum Take Off Weight

Maximum Landing Weight

Launched in:_____ Based on:_____
First Flight: _____ Entry Into Service: _____

———Basic Operation Data———

Engine Information:_____
_____

Transport Capacity:_____
_____

Range: _____
_____

———— Aircraft Spotted ————

Date/Time Spotted _____

Where/Location   _____

Airport Details   _____

_____

Notes

_____
_____
_____
_____

Aircraft Name_____

Aircraft Dimensions
Overall Length:

Height:

Fuselage Diameter:

Wingspan:

Wing Area:

Design Weight

Maximum Take Off Weight

Maximum Landing Weight

Launched in:_____ Based on:_____
First Flight: _____ Entry Into Service: _____

———— Basic Operation Data ————
Engine Information:_____
_____

Transport Capacity:_____
_____

Range: _____
_____

———— Aircraft Spotted ————
Date/Time Spotted _____

Where/Location   _____

Airport Details   _____

_____

Notes
_____
_____
_____
_____

Aircraft Name_____

Aircraft Dimensions
Overall Length:

Height:

Fuselage Diameter:

Wingspan:

Wing Area:

Design Weight

Maximum Take Off Weight

Maximum Landing Weight

Launched in:_____ Based on:_____
First Flight: _____ Entry Into Service: _____

————— Basic Operation Data —————

Engine Information:_____
_____

Transport Capacity:_____
_____

Range:_____
_____

————— Aircraft Spotted —————

Date/Time Spotted_____

Where/Location _____

Airport Details _____

Notes
_____
_____
_____
_____

Aircraft Name_____

Aircraft Dimensions   Design Weight

Overall Length:

Height: Maximum Take Off Weight

Fuselage Diameter:

Wingspan:
                                                                Maximum Landing Weight
Wing Area:

Launched in:_____ Based on:_____
First Flight: _____ Entry Into Service: _____

──────── Basic Operation Data ────────

Engine Information:_____
_____

Transport Capacity:_____
_____

Range: _____
_____

──────── Aircraft Spotted ────────

Date/Time Spotted _____

Where/Location   _____

Airport Details   _____
_____

Notes
_____
_____
_____
_____

Aircraft Name _____

Aircraft Dimensions
Overall Length:

Height:

Fuselage Diameter:

Wingspan:

Wing Area:

Design Weight

Maximum Take Off Weight

Maximum Landing Weight

Launched in:_____ Based on:_____
First Flight: _____ Entry Into Service: _____

———————Basic Operation Data———————

Engine Information:_____
_____

Transport Capacity:_____
_____

Range: _____
_____

————— Aircraft Spotted —————

Date/Time Spotted_____

Where/Location   _____

Airport Details   _____

_____

Notes

_____
_____
_____
_____

Aircraft Name _____

Aircraft Dimensions

Overall Length:

Height:

Fuselage Diameter:

Wingspan:

Wing Area:

Design Weight

Maximum Take Off Weight

Maximum Landing Weight

Launched in: _____ Based on: _____
First Flight: _____ Entry Into Service: _____

——————— Basic Operation Data ———————

Engine Information: _____
_____

Transport Capacity: _____
_____

Range: _____
_____

——————— Aircraft Spotted ———————

Date/Time Spotted _____

Where/Location   _____

Airport Details   _____

_____

Notes
_____
_____
_____
_____

Aircraft Name_____

Aircraft Dimensions

Overall Length:

Height:

Fuselage Diameter:

Wingspan:

Wing Area:

Design Weight

Maximum Take Off Weight

Maximum Landing Weight

Launched in:_____ Based on:_____
First Flight: _____ Entry Into Service: _____

————— Basic Operation Data —————

Engine Information:_____
_____

Transport Capacity:_____
_____

Range: _____
_____

————— Aircraft Spotted —————

Date/Time Spotted_____

Where/Location _____

Airport Details _____
_____

Notes

_____
_____
_____

Aircraft Name _____

Aircraft Dimensions

Overall **Length**:

Height:

Fuselage Diameter:

Wingspan:

Wing Area:

Design Weight

Maximum Take Off Weight

Maximum Landing Weight

Launched in: _____ Based on: _____
First Flight: _____ Entry Into Service: _____

──────── Basic Operation Data ────────

Engine Information: _____
_____

Transport Capacity: _____
_____

Range: _____
_____

──────── Aircraft Spotted ────────

Date/Time Spotted _____

Where/Location   _____

Airport Details _____

Notes
_____
_____
_____
_____

Aircraft Name _____

Aircraft Dimensions
Overall Length:

Height:

Fuselage Diameter:

Wingspan:

Wing Area:

Design Weight

Maximum Take Off Weight

Maximum Landing Weight

Launched in: _____ Based on: _____
First Flight: _____ Entry Into Service: _____

——————— Basic Operation Data ———————
Engine Information: _____
_____

Transport Capacity: _____
_____

Range: _____
_____

——————— Aircraft Spotted ———————
Date/Time Spotted _____

Where/Location   _____

Airport Details   _____
_____

Notes
_____
_____
_____
_____

Aircraft Name _____

Aircraft Dimensions
Overall **Length:**

Height:

Fuselage Diameter:

Wingspan:

Wing Area:

Design Weight

Maximum Take Off Weight

Maximum Landing Weight

Launched in: _____ Based on: _____
First Flight: _____ Entry Into Service: _____

———— Basic Operation Data ————
Engine Information: _____
_____

Transport Capacity: _____
_____

Range: _____
_____

———— Aircraft Spotted ————
Date/Time Spotted _____

Where/Location _____

Airport Details _____

Notes
_____
_____
_____
_____

Aircraft Name_____

Aircraft Dimensions

Overall Length:

Height:

Fuselage Diameter:

Wingspan:

Wing Area:

Design Weight

Maximum Take Off Weight

Maximum Landing Weight

Launched in:_____ Based on:_____
First Flight: _____ Entry Into Service: _____

———————Basic Operation Data———————

Engine Information:_____

_____

Transport Capacity:_____

_____

Range:_____

_____

————————— Aircraft Spotted —————————

Date/Time Spotted_____

Where/Location   _____

Airport Details   _____

_____

Notes

_____
_____
_____
_____

Aircraft Name _____

Aircraft Dimensions

Overall **Length**:

Height:

Fuselage Diameter:

Wingspan:

Wing Area:

Design Weight

Maximum Take Off Weight

Maximum Landing Weight

Launched in: _____ Based on: _____
First Flight: _____ Entry Into Service: _____

——— Basic Operation Data ———

Engine Information: _____
_____

Transport Capacity: _____
_____

Range: _____
_____

——— Aircraft Spotted ———

Date/Time Spotted _____

Where/Location _____

Airport Details _____

Notes
_____
_____
_____
_____

Aircraft Name_____

Aircraft Dimensions

Overall Length:

Height:

Fuselage Diameter:

Wingspan:

Wing Area:

Design Weight

Maximum Take Off Weight

Maximum Landing Weight

Launched in:_____ Based on:_____
First Flight: _____ Entry Into Service: _____

—————Basic Operation Data—————

Engine Information:_____
_____

Transport Capacity:_____
_____

Range: _____
_____

————— Aircraft Spotted —————

Date/Time Spotted _____

Where/Location   _____

Airport Details   _____

Notes
_____
_____
_____
_____

Aircraft Name_____

Aircraft Dimensions

Overall **Length:**

Height:

Fuselage Diameter:

Wingspan:

Wing Area:

Design Weight

Maximum Take Off Weight

Maximum Landing Weight

Launched in:_____ Based on:_____
First Flight: _____ Entry Into Service: _____

———————Basic Operation Data———————

Engine Information:_____
_____

Transport Capacity:_____
_____

Range: _____
_____

——————— Aircraft Spotted ———————

Date/Time Spotted_____

Where/Location   _____

Airport Details   _____

_____

Notes

_____
_____
_____
_____

Aircraft Name_____

Aircraft Dimensions

Overall Length:

Height:

Fuselage Diameter:

Wingspan:

Wing Area:

Design Weight

Maximum Take Off Weight

Maximum Landing Weight

Launched in:_____ Based on:_____
First Flight: _____ Entry Into Service: _____

———— Basic Operation Data ————

Engine Information:_____
_____

Transport Capacity:_____
_____

Range:_____
_____

———— Aircraft Spotted ————

Date/Time Spotted_____

Where/Location   _____

Airport Details   _____

Notes
_____
_____
_____
_____

Aircraft Name_____

Aircraft Dimensions

Overall **Length:**

Height:

Fuselage Diameter:

Wingspan:

Wing Area:

Design Weight

Maximum Take Off Weight

Maximum Landing Weight

Launched in:_____ Based on:_____
First Flight: _____ Entry Into Service: _____

————Basic Operation Data————

Engine Information:_____
_____

Transport Capacity:_____
_____

Range: _____
_____

————— Aircraft Spotted —————

Date/Time Spotted _____

Where/Location   _____

Airport Details   _____
_____

Notes
_____
_____
_____
_____

Aircraft Name_____

Aircraft Dimensions

Overall Length:

Height:

Fuselage Diameter:

Wingspan:

Wing Area:

Design Weight

Maximum Take Off Weight

Maximum Landing Weight

Launched in:_____ Based on:_____
First Flight: _____ Entry Into Service: _____

———————Basic Operation Data———————

Engine Information:_____
_____

Transport Capacity:_____
_____

Range: _____
_____

——————— Aircraft Spotted ———————

Date/Time Spotted_____

Where/Location   _____

Airport Details   _____

_____

Notes
_____
_____
_____
_____

Aircraft Name_____

Aircraft Dimensions
Overall Length:

Height:

Fuselage Diameter:

Wingspan:

Wing Area:

Design Weight

Maximum Take Off Weight

Maximum Landing Weight

Launched in:_____ Based on:_____
First Flight: _____ Entry Into Service: _____

————Basic Operation Data————

Engine Information:_____
_____

Transport Capacity:_____
_____

Range: _____
_____

———— Aircraft Spotted ————

Date/Time Spotted_____

Where/Location   _____

Airport Details   _____
_____

Notes
_____
_____
_____
_____

Aircraft Name_____

Aircraft Dimensions
Overall Length:

Height:

Fuselage Diameter:

Wingspan:

Wing Area:

Design Weight

Maximum Take Off Weight

Maximum Landing Weight

Launched in:_____ Based on:_____
First Flight: _____ Entry Into Service: _____

————— Basic Operation Data —————

Engine Information:_____
_____

Transport Capacity:_____
_____

Range: _____
_____

————— Aircraft Spotted —————

Date/Time Spotted _____

Where/Location   _____

Airport Details   _____

Notes
_____
_____
_____
_____

Aircraft Name _____

Aircraft Dimensions

Overall **Length**:

Height:

Fuselage Diameter:

Wingspan:

Wing Area:

Design Weight

Maximum Take Off Weight

Maximum Landing Weight

Launched in: _____ Based on: _____
First Flight: _____ Entry Into Service: _____

———— Basic Operation Data ————

Engine Information: _____
_____

Transport Capacity: _____
_____

Range: _____
_____

———— Aircraft Spotted ————

Date/Time Spotted _____

Where/Location _____

Airport Details _____

_____

Notes

_____
_____
_____
_____

Aircraft Name_____

Aircraft Dimensions

Overall Length:

Height:

Fuselage Diameter:

Wingspan:

Wing Area:

Design Weight

Maximum Take Off Weight

Maximum Landing Weight

Launched in:_____ Based on:_____
First Flight: _____ Entry Into Service: _____

———— Basic Operation Data ————

Engine Information:_____

_____

Transport Capacity:_____

_____

Range:_____

_____

———— Aircraft Spotted ————

Date/Time Spotted_____

Where/Location   _____

Airport Details   _____

_____

Notes

_____
_____
_____
_____

Aircraft Name_____

Aircraft Dimensions
Overall **Length:**

Height:

Fuselage Diameter:

Wingspan:

Wing Area:

Design Weight

Maximum Take Off Weight

Maximum Landing Weight

Launched in:_____ Based on:_____
First Flight: _____ Entry Into Service: _____

———————Basic Operation Data———————

Engine Information:_____
_____

Transport Capacity:_____
_____

Range: _____
_____

——————— Aircraft Spotted ———————

Date/Time Spotted _____

Where/Location   _____

Airport Details   _____
_____

Notes
_____
_____
_____
_____

Aircraft Name_____

Aircraft Dimensions
Overall Length:

Height:

Fuselage Diameter:

Wingspan:

Wing Area:

Design Weight

Maximum Take Off Weight

Maximum Landing Weight

Launched in:_____ Based on:_____
First Flight: _____ Entry Into Service: _____

———— Basic Operation Data ————
Engine Information:_____
_____

Transport Capacity:_____
_____

Range: _____
_____

———— Aircraft Spotted ————
Date/Time Spotted_____

Where/Location   _____

Airport Details   _____

_____

Notes
_____
_____
_____

Aircraft Name _____

Aircraft Dimensions   Design Weight

Overall **Length**:

Height: Maximum Take Off Weight

Fuselage Diameter:

Wingspan: Maximum Landing Weight

Wing Area:

Launched in:_____ Based on:_____
First Flight: _____ Entry Into Service: _____

─────── Basic Operation Data ───────

Engine Information:_____
_____

Transport Capacity:_____
_____

Range:_____
_____

─────── Aircraft Spotted ───────

Date/Time Spotted _____

Where/Location   _____

Airport Details   _____
_____

Notes
_____
_____
_____
_____

Aircraft Name_____

Aircraft Dimensions

Overall Length:

Height:

Fuselage Diameter:

Wingspan:

Wing Area:

Design Weight

Maximum Take Off Weight

Maximum Landing Weight

Launched in:_____ Based on:_____
First Flight: _____ Entry Into Service: _____

——————Basic Operation Data——————

Engine Information:_____
_____

Transport Capacity:_____
_____

Range: _____
_____

—————— Aircraft Spotted ——————

Date/Time Spotted_____

Where/Location _____

Airport Details _____

Notes
_____
_____
_____
_____

Aircraft Name _____

Aircraft Dimensions
Overall **Length:**

Height:

Fuselage Diameter:

Wingspan:

Wing Area:

Design Weight

Maximum Take Off Weight

Maximum Landing Weight

Launched in:_____ Based on:_____
First Flight: _____ Entry Into Service: _____

———— Basic Operation Data ————
Engine Information:_____
_____

Transport Capacity:_____
_____

Range: _____
_____

———— Aircraft Spotted ————
Date/Time Spotted _____

Where/Location   _____

Airport Details   _____
_____

Notes
_____
_____
_____
_____

Aircraft Name_____

Aircraft Dimensions　　　　　Design Weight

Overall Length:

Height:　　　　　　　　　　Maximum Take Off Weight

Fuselage Diameter:

Wingspan:
　　　　　　　　　　　　　　　Maximum Landing Weight
Wing Area:

Launched in:_____ Based on:_____
First Flight: _____ Entry Into Service: _____

———Basic Operation Data———

Engine Information:_____
_____

Transport Capacity:_____
_____

Range:_____
_____

——— Aircraft Spotted ———

Date/Time Spotted _____

Where/Location　　_____

Airport Details　　 _____

Notes
_____
_____
_____
_____

Aircraft Name _____

Aircraft Dimensions

Overall **Length:**

Height:

Fuselage Diameter:

Wingspan:

Wing Area:

Design Weight

Maximum Take Off Weight

Maximum Landing Weight

Launched in: _____ Based on: _____
First Flight: _____ Entry Into Service: _____

———— Basic Operation Data ————

Engine Information: _____
_____

Transport Capacity: _____
_____

Range: _____
_____

———— Aircraft Spotted ————

Date/Time Spotted _____

Where/Location   _____

Airport Details   _____

_____

Notes
_____
_____
_____
_____

Aircraft Name_____

Aircraft Dimensions
Overall Length:

Height:

Fuselage Diameter:

Wingspan:

Wing Area:

Design Weight

Maximum Take Off Weight

Maximum Landing Weight

Launched in:_____ Based on:_____
First Flight: _____ Entry Into Service: _____

──────── Basic Operation Data ────────

Engine Information:_____

_____

Transport Capacity:_____

_____

Range: _____

_____

──────── Aircraft Spotted ────────

Date/Time Spotted _____

Where/Location   _____

Airport Details   _____

_____

Notes

_____
_____
_____
_____

Aircraft Name_____

Aircraft Dimensions

Overall **Length:**

Height:

Fuselage Diameter:

Wingspan:

Wing Area:

Design Weight

Maximum Take Off Weight

Maximum Landing Weight

Launched in:_____ Based on:_____
First Flight: _____ Entry Into Service: _____

———— Basic Operation Data ————

Engine Information:_____
_____

Transport Capacity:_____
_____

Range:_____
_____

———— Aircraft Spotted ————

Date/Time Spotted_____

Where/Location   _____

Airport Details   _____
_____

Notes
_____
_____
_____
_____

Aircraft Name_____

Aircraft Dimensions
Overall Length:

Height:

Fuselage Diameter:

Wingspan:

Wing Area:

Design Weight

Maximum Take Off Weight

Maximum Landing Weight

Launched in:_____ Based on:_____
First Flight: _____ Entry Into Service: _____

——————Basic Operation Data——————
Engine Information:_____
_____

Transport Capacity:_____
_____

Range: _____
_____

—————— Aircraft Spotted ——————
Date/Time Spotted_____

Where/Location _____

Airport Details   _____

Notes
_____
_____
_____
_____

Aircraft Name _____

Aircraft Dimensions
Overall Length:

Height:

Fuselage Diameter:

Wingspan:

Wing Area:

Design Weight

Maximum Take Off Weight

Maximum Landing Weight

Launched in: _____ Based on: _____
First Flight: _____ Entry Into Service: _____

———— Basic Operation Data ————

Engine Information: _____
_____

Transport Capacity: _____
_____

Range: _____
_____

———— Aircraft Spotted ————

Date/Time Spotted _____

Where/Location _____

Airport Details _____

_____

Notes

_____
_____
_____
_____

Aircraft Name_____

Aircraft Dimensions
Overall Length:

Height:

Fuselage Diameter:

Wingspan:

Wing Area:

Design Weight

Maximum Take Off Weight

Maximum Landing Weight

Launched in:_____ Based on:_____
First Flight: _____ Entry Into Service: _____

————Basic Operation Data————

Engine Information:_____
_____

Transport Capacity:_____
_____

Range:_____
_____

———— Aircraft Spotted ————

Date/Time Spotted _____

Where/Location _____

Airport Details _____

_____

Notes
_____
_____
_____
_____

Aircraft Name_____

Aircraft Dimensions

Overall **Length**:

Height:

Fuselage Diameter:

Wingspan:

Wing Area:

Design Weight

Maximum Take Off Weight

Maximum Landing Weight

Launched in:_____ Based on:_____
First Flight: _____ Entry Into Service: _____

———————Basic Operation Data———————

Engine Information:_____
_____

Transport Capacity:_____
_____

Range:_____
_____

——————— Aircraft Spotted ———————

Date/Time Spotted_____

Where/Location   _____

Airport Details   _____
_____

Notes
_____
_____
_____
_____

Aircraft Name_____

Aircraft Dimensions

Overall Length:

Height:

Fuselage Diameter:

Wingspan:

Wing Area:

Design Weight

Maximum Take Off Weight

Maximum Landing Weight

Launched in:_____ Based on:_____
First Flight: _____ Entry Into Service: _____

——————Basic Operation Data——————

Engine Information:_____
_____

Transport Capacity:_____
_____

Range: _____
_____

—————— Aircraft Spotted ——————

Date/Time Spotted_____

Where/Location   _____

Airport Details   _____

Notes

_____
_____
_____
_____

Aircraft Name_____

Aircraft Dimensions
Overall Length:

Height:

Fuselage Diameter:

Wingspan:

Wing Area:

Design Weight

Maximum Take Off Weight

Maximum Landing Weight

Launched in:_____ Based on:_____
First Flight: _____ Entry Into Service: _____

————— Basic Operation Data —————

Engine Information:_____
_____

Transport Capacity:_____
_____

Range: _____
_____

————— Aircraft Spotted —————

Date/Time Spotted_____

Where/Location _____

Airport Details _____

Notes
_____
_____
_____
_____

Aircraft Name_____

Aircraft Dimensions
Overall Length:

Height:

Fuselage Diameter:

Wingspan:

Wing Area:

Design Weight

Maximum Take Off Weight

Maximum Landing Weight

Launched in:_____ Based on:_____
First Flight: _____ Entry Into Service: _____

————Basic Operation Data————
Engine Information:_____
_____

Transport Capacity:_____
_____

Range:_____
_____

———— Aircraft Spotted ————
Date/Time Spotted_____

Where/Location   _____

Airport Details   _____

_____

Notes
_____
_____
_____
_____

Aircraft Name _____

Aircraft Dimensions

Overall Length:

Height:

Fuselage Diameter:

Wingspan:

Wing Area:

Design Weight

Maximum Take Off Weight

Maximum Landing Weight

Launched in: _____ Based on: _____
First Flight: _____ Entry Into Service: _____

———— Basic Operation Data ————

Engine Information: _____
_____

Transport Capacity: _____
_____

Range: _____
_____

———— Aircraft Spotted ————

Date/Time Spotted _____

Where/Location _____

Airport Details _____

_____

Notes

_____
_____
_____
_____

Aircraft Name_____

Aircraft Dimensions
Overall Length:

Height:

Fuselage Diameter:

Wingspan:

Wing Area:

Design Weight

Maximum Take Off Weight

Maximum Landing Weight

Launched in:_____ Based on:_____
First Flight: _____ Entry Into Service: _____

——————Basic Operation Data——————

Engine Information:_____
_____

Transport Capacity:_____
_____

Range:_____
_____

—————— Aircraft Spotted ——————

Date/Time Spotted _____

Where/Location   _____

Airport Details   _____

_____

Notes
_____
_____
_____
_____

Aircraft Name _____

Aircraft Dimensions

Overall **Length:**

Height:

Fuselage Diameter:

Wingspan:

Wing Area:

Design Weight

Maximum Take Off Weight

Maximum Landing Weight

Launched in: _____ Based on: _____
First Flight: _____ Entry Into Service: _____

———— Basic Operation Data ————

Engine Information: _____
_____

Transport Capacity: _____
_____

Range: _____
_____

———— Aircraft Spotted ————

Date/Time Spotted _____

Where/Location _____

Airport Details _____

_____

Notes
_____
_____
_____
_____

Aircraft Name_____

Aircraft Dimensions   Design Weight

Overall Length:

Height: Maximum Take Off Weight

Fuselage Diameter:

Wingspan: Maximum Landing Weight

Wing Area:

Launched in:_____ Based on:_____
First Flight: _____ Entry Into Service: _____

———— Basic Operation Data ————

Engine Information:_____
_____

Transport Capacity:_____
_____

Range: _____
_____

———— Aircraft Spotted ————

Date/Time Spotted_____
Where/Location   _____
Airport Details   _____
_____

Notes
_____
_____
_____
_____

Aircraft Name_____

Aircraft Dimensions

Overall **Length**:

Height:

Fuselage Diameter:

Wingspan:

Wing Area:

Design Weight

Maximum Take Off Weight

Maximum Landing Weight

Launched in:_____ Based on:_____
First Flight: _____ Entry Into Service: _____

———————Basic Operation Data———————

Engine Information:_____
_____

Transport Capacity:_____
_____

Range:_____
_____

——————— Aircraft Spotted ———————

Date/Time Spotted_____

Where/Location   _____

Airport Details   _____
_____

Notes
_____
_____
_____
_____

Aircraft Name_____

Aircraft Dimensions   Design Weight
Overall Length:

Height: Maximum Take Off Weight

Fuselage Diameter:

Wingspan:
                                         Maximum Landing Weight
Wing Area:

Launched in:_____ Based on:_____
First Flight: _____ Entry Into Service: _____

————Basic Operation Data————
Engine Information:_____
_____

Transport Capacity:_____
_____

Range: _____
_____

———— Aircraft Spotted ————
Date/Time Spotted_____
Where/Location   _____
Airport Details   _____

_____
Notes
_____
_____
_____
_____

Aircraft Name_____

Aircraft Dimensions
Overall **Length**:

Height:

Fuselage Diameter:

Wingspan:

Wing Area:

Design Weight

Maximum Take Off Weight

Maximum Landing Weight

Launched in:_____ Based on:_____
First Flight: _____ Entry Into Service: _____

————Basic Operation Data————
Engine Information:_____
_____

Transport Capacity:_____
_____

Range: _____
_____

———— Aircraft Spotted ————
Date/Time Spotted_____

Where/Location   _____

Airport Details   _____
_____

Notes
_____
_____
_____
_____

Aircraft Name _____

Aircraft Dimensions
Overall Length:

Height:

Fuselage Diameter:

Wingspan:

Wing Area:

Design Weight

Maximum Take Off Weight

Maximum Landing Weight

Launched in: _____ Based on: _____
First Flight: _____ Entry Into Service: _____

──────── Basic Operation Data ────────

Engine Information: _____

_____

Transport Capacity: _____

_____

Range: _____

_____

────── Aircraft Spotted ──────

Date/Time Spotted _____

Where/Location   _____

Airport Details   _____

_____

Notes
_____
_____
_____
_____

Aircraft Name _____

Aircraft Dimensions

Overall **Length:**

Height:

Fuselage Diameter:

Wingspan:

Wing Area:

Design Weight

Maximum Take Off Weight

Maximum Landing Weight

Launched in: _____ Based on: _____
First Flight: _____ Entry Into Service: _____

——————— Basic Operation Data ———————

Engine Information: _____
_____

Transport Capacity: _____
_____

Range: _____
_____

——————— Aircraft Spotted ———————

Date/Time Spotted _____

Where/Location   _____

Airport Details   _____

Notes
_____
_____
_____

Aircraft Name_____

Aircraft Dimensions

Overall Length:

Height:

Fuselage Diameter:

Wingspan:

Wing Area:

Design Weight

Maximum Take Off Weight

Maximum Landing Weight

Launched in:_____ Based on:_____
First Flight: _____ Entry Into Service: _____

──────── Basic Operation Data ────────

Engine Information:_____
_____

Transport Capacity:_____
_____

Range: _____
_____

────── Aircraft Spotted ──────

Date/Time Spotted_____

Where/Location   _____

Airport Details   _____

Notes

_____
_____
_____
_____

Aircraft Name_____

Aircraft Dimensions

Overall Length:

Height:

Fuselage Diameter:

Wingspan:

Wing Area:

Design Weight

Maximum Take Off Weight

Maximum Landing Weight

Launched in:_____ Based on:_____
First Flight: _____ Entry Into Service: _____

———— Basic Operation Data ————

Engine Information:_____
_____

Transport Capacity:_____
_____

Range:_____
_____

———— Aircraft Spotted ————

Date/Time Spotted _____

Where/Location _____

Airport Details   _____

Notes
_____
_____
_____
_____

Aircraft Name _____

Aircraft Dimensions

Overall Length:

Height:

Fuselage Diameter:

Wingspan:

Wing Area:

Design Weight

Maximum Take Off Weight

Maximum Landing Weight

Launched in: _____ Based on: _____
First Flight: _____ Entry Into Service: _____

———— Basic Operation Data ————

Engine Information: _____
_____

Transport Capacity: _____
_____

Range: _____
_____

———— Aircraft Spotted ————

Date/Time Spotted _____

Where/Location   _____

Airport Details   _____

Notes
_____
_____
_____

Aircraft Name_____

Aircraft Dimensions

Overall Length:

Height:

Fuselage Diameter:

Wingspan:

Wing Area:

Design Weight

Maximum Take Off Weight

Maximum Landing Weight

Launched in:_____ Based on:_____
First Flight: _____ Entry Into Service: _____

———————— Basic Operation Data ————————

Engine Information:_____
_____

Transport Capacity:_____
_____

Range:_____
_____

——————— Aircraft Spotted ———————

Date/Time Spotted _____

Where/Location   _____

Airport Details   _____
_____

Notes

_____
_____
_____
_____

Aircraft Name _____

Aircraft Dimensions
Overall **Length:**

Height:

Fuselage Diameter:

Wingspan:

Wing Area:

Design Weight

Maximum Take Off Weight

Maximum Landing Weight

Launched in:_____ Based on:_____
First Flight: _____ Entry Into Service: _____

———— Basic Operation Data ————
Engine Information:_____
_____

Transport Capacity:_____
_____

Range:_____
_____

———— Aircraft Spotted ————
Date/Time Spotted _____

Where/Location _____

Airport Details _____

_____

Notes

_____
_____
_____
_____

Aircraft Name _____

Aircraft Dimensions

Overall **Length:**

Height:

Fuselage Diameter:

Wingspan:

Wing Area:

Design Weight

Maximum Take Off Weight

Maximum Landing Weight

Launched in: _____ Based on: _____
First Flight: _____ Entry Into Service: _____

———— Basic Operation Data ————

Engine Information: _____
_____

Transport Capacity: _____
_____

Range: _____
_____

———— Aircraft Spotted ————

Date/Time Spotted _____

Where/Location _____

Airport Details _____

_____

Notes
_____
_____
_____
_____

Aircraft Name _____

Aircraft Dimensions

Overall Length:

Height:

Fuselage Diameter:

Wingspan:

Wing Area:

Design Weight

Maximum Take Off Weight

Maximum Landing Weight

Launched in: _____ Based on: _____
First Flight: _____ Entry Into Service: _____

———— Basic Operation Data ————

Engine Information: _____

Transport Capacity: _____

Range: _____

———— Aircraft Spotted ————

Date/Time Spotted _____

Where/Location _____

Airport Details _____

Notes
_____
_____
_____
_____

Aircraft Name _____

Aircraft Dimensions
Overall Length:

Height:

Fuselage Diameter:

Wingspan:

Wing Area:

Design Weight

Maximum Take Off Weight

Maximum Landing Weight

Launched in: _____ Based on: _____
First Flight: _____ Entry Into Service: _____

——————— Basic Operation Data ———————
Engine Information: _____
_____

Transport Capacity: _____
_____

Range: _____
_____

——————— Aircraft Spotted ———————
Date/Time Spotted _____

Where/Location _____

Airport Details _____

Notes
_____
_____
_____
_____

Aircraft Name_____

Aircraft Dimensions

Overall Length:

Height:

Fuselage Diameter:

Wingspan:

Wing Area:

Design Weight

Maximum Take Off Weight

Maximum Landing Weight

Launched in:_____ Based on:_____
First Flight: _____ Entry Into Service: _____

——————Basic Operation Data——————

Engine Information:_____
_____

Transport Capacity:_____
_____

Range: _____
_____

—————— Aircraft Spotted ——————

Date/Time Spotted_____

Where/Location   _____

Airport Details   _____

_____

Notes

_____
_____
_____
_____

Aircraft Name_____

Aircraft Dimensions

Overall **Length:**

Height:

Fuselage Diameter:

Wingspan:

Wing Area:

Design Weight

Maximum Take Off Weight

Maximum Landing Weight

Launched in:_____ Based on:_____
First Flight: _____ Entry Into Service: _____

——————Basic Operation Data——————

Engine Information:_____
_____

Transport Capacity:_____
_____

Range: _____
_____

————— Aircraft Spotted —————

Date/Time Spotted_____

Where/Location   _____

Airport Details   _____

_____

Notes

_____
_____
_____
_____

Aircraft Name _____

Aircraft Dimensions

Overall Length:

Height:

Fuselage Diameter:

Wingspan:

Wing Area:

Design Weight

Maximum Take Off Weight

Maximum Landing Weight

Launched in: _____ Based on: _____
First Flight: _____ Entry Into Service: _____

———— Basic Operation Data ————

Engine Information: _____
_____

Transport Capacity: _____
_____

Range: _____
_____

———— Aircraft Spotted ————

Date/Time Spotted _____

Where/Location   _____

Airport Details   _____

Notes
_____
_____
_____
_____

Aircraft Name_____

Aircraft Dimensions
Overall **Length:**

Height:

Fuselage Diameter:

Wingspan:

Wing Area:

Design Weight

Maximum Take Off Weight

Maximum Landing Weight

Launched in:_____ Based on:_____
First Flight: _____ Entry Into Service: _____

———————Basic Operation Data———————
Engine Information:_____
_____

Transport Capacity:_____
_____

Range:_____
_____

——————— Aircraft Spotted ———————
Date/Time Spotted_____

Where/Location   _____

Airport Details   _____

_____

Notes
_____
_____
_____
_____

Aircraft Name_____

Aircraft Dimensions   Design Weight

Overall Length:

Height: Maximum Take Off Weight

Fuselage Diameter:

Wingspan: Maximum Landing Weight

Wing Area:

Launched in:_____ Based on:_____
First Flight: _____ Entry Into Service: _____

———— Basic Operation Data ————

Engine Information:_____
_____

Transport Capacity:_____
_____

Range: _____
_____

———— Aircraft Spotted ————

Date/Time Spotted_____
Where/Location   _____
Airport Details   _____
_____

Notes
_____
_____
_____
_____

Aircraft Name _____

Aircraft Dimensions

Overall **Length**:

Height:

Fuselage Diameter:

Wingspan:

Wing Area:

Design Weight

Maximum Take Off Weight

Maximum Landing Weight

Launched in: _____ Based on: _____
First Flight: _____ Entry Into Service: _____

———— Basic Operation Data ————

Engine Information: _____
_____

Transport Capacity: _____
_____

Range: _____
_____

———— Aircraft Spotted ————

Date/Time Spotted _____

Where/Location _____

Airport Details _____

_____

Notes
_____
_____
_____
_____

Aircraft Name_____

Aircraft Dimensions

Overall Length:

Height:

Fuselage Diameter:

Wingspan:

Wing Area:

Design Weight

Maximum Take Off Weight

Maximum Landing Weight

Launched in:_____ Based on:_____
First Flight: _____ Entry Into Service: _____

———————Basic Operation Data———————

Engine Information:_____
_____

Transport Capacity:_____
_____

Range: _____
_____

——————— Aircraft Spotted ———————

Date/Time Spotted_____

Where/Location   _____

Airport Details   _____

Notes

_____
_____
_____
_____

Aircraft Name _____

Aircraft Dimensions
Overall **Length:**

Height:

Fuselage Diameter:

Wingspan:

Wing Area:

Design Weight

Maximum Take Off Weight

Maximum Landing Weight

Launched in:_____ Based on:_____
First Flight: _____ Entry Into Service: _____

─────── Basic Operation Data ───────
Engine Information:_____
_____

Transport Capacity:_____
_____

Range: _____
_____

─────── Aircraft Spotted ───────
Date/Time Spotted _____

Where/Location _____

Airport Details _____
_____

Notes
_____
_____
_____
_____

Aircraft Name_____

Aircraft Dimensions   Design Weight

Overall Length:

Height: Maximum Take Off Weight

Fuselage Diameter:

Wingspan: Maximum Landing Weight

Wing Area:

Launched in:_____ Based on:_____
First Flight: _____ Entry Into Service: _____

——————— Basic Operation Data ———————

Engine Information:_____
_____

Transport Capacity:_____
_____

Range:_____
_____

——————— Aircraft Spotted ———————

Date/Time Spotted_____
Where/Location   _____
Airport Details   _____
_____

Notes

_____
_____
_____
_____

Aircraft Name_____

Aircraft Dimensions   Design Weight

Overall Length:

Height: Maximum Take Off Weight

Fuselage Diameter:

Wingspan: Maximum Landing Weight

Wing Area:

Launched in:_____ Based on:_____
First Flight: _____ Entry Into Service: _____

————Basic Operation Data————

Engine Information:_____
_____

Transport Capacity:_____
_____

Range: _____
_____

————— Aircraft Spotted —————

Date/Time Spotted_____

Where/Location   _____

Airport Details   _____

_____
                        Notes
_____
_____
_____
_____

Aircraft Name_____

Aircraft Dimensions

Overall Length:

Height:

Fuselage Diameter:

Wingspan:

Wing Area:

Design Weight

Maximum Take Off Weight

Maximum Landing Weight

Launched in:_____ Based on:_____
First Flight: _____ Entry Into Service: _____

————— Basic Operation Data —————

Engine Information:_____
_____

Transport Capacity:_____
_____

Range: _____
_____

————— Aircraft Spotted —————

Date/Time Spotted_____

Where/Location   _____

Airport Details _____

Notes
_____
_____
_____
_____

Aircraft Name_____

Aircraft Dimensions
Overall Length:

Height:

Fuselage Diameter:

Wingspan:

Wing Area:

Design Weight

Maximum Take Off Weight

Maximum Landing Weight

Launched in:_____ Based on:_____
First Flight: _____ Entry Into Service: _____

————Basic Operation Data————
Engine Information:_____
_____

Transport Capacity:_____
_____

Range: _____
_____

———— Aircraft Spotted ————
Date/Time Spotted _____

Where/Location _____

Airport Details _____

_____

Notes
_____
_____
_____
_____

Aircraft Name_____

Aircraft Dimensions

Overall Length:

Height:

Fuselage Diameter:

Wingspan:

Wing Area:

Design Weight

Maximum Take Off Weight

Maximum Landing Weight

Launched in:_____ Based on:_____
First Flight: _____ Entry Into Service: _____

————— Basic Operation Data —————

Engine Information:_____

Transport Capacity:_____

Range:_____

————— Aircraft Spotted —————

Date/Time Spotted_____

Where/Location _____

Airport Details _____

Notes

Aircraft Name_____

Aircraft Dimensions
Overall Length:

Height:

Fuselage Diameter:

Wingspan:

Wing Area:

Design Weight

Maximum Take Off Weight

Maximum Landing Weight

Launched in:_____ Based on:_____
First Flight: _____ Entry Into Service: _____

——————Basic Operation Data——————
Engine Information:_____
_____

Transport Capacity:_____
_____

Range: _____
_____

—————— Aircraft Spotted ——————
Date/Time Spotted _____

Where/Location   _____

Airport Details   _____
_____

Notes
_____
_____
_____
_____

Aircraft Name _____

Aircraft Dimensions
Overall Length:

Height:

Fuselage Diameter:

Wingspan:

Wing Area:

Design Weight

Maximum Take Off Weight

Maximum Landing Weight

Launched in: _____ Based on: _____
First Flight: _____ Entry Into Service: _____

──────── Basic Operation Data ────────
Engine Information: _____
_____

Transport Capacity: _____
_____

Range: _____
_____

──────── Aircraft Spotted ────────
Date/Time Spotted _____

Where/Location _____

Airport Details _____

_____
Notes
_____
_____
_____

Aircraft Name _____

Aircraft Dimensions

Overall **Length:**

Height:

Fuselage Diameter:

Wingspan:

Wing Area:

Design Weight

Maximum Take Off Weight

Maximum Landing Weight

Launched in: _____ Based on: _____
First Flight: _____ Entry Into Service: _____

———— Basic Operation Data ————

Engine Information: _____
_____

Transport Capacity: _____
_____

Range: _____
_____

———— Aircraft Spotted ————

Date/Time Spotted _____

Where/Location   _____

Airport Details   _____

_____

Notes
_____
_____
_____
_____

Aircraft Name_____

Aircraft Dimensions

Overall Length:

Height:

Fuselage Diameter:

Wingspan:

Wing Area:

Design Weight

Maximum Take Off Weight

Maximum Landing Weight

Launched in:_____ Based on:_____
First Flight: _____ Entry Into Service: _____

———— Basic Operation Data ————

Engine Information:_____
_____

Transport Capacity:_____
_____

Range: _____
_____

———— Aircraft Spotted ————

Date/Time Spotted _____

Where/Location _____

Airport Details _____
_____

Notes
_____
_____
_____
_____

Aircraft Name _____

Aircraft Dimensions

Overall Length:

Height:

Fuselage Diameter:

Wingspan:

Wing Area:

Design Weight

Maximum Take Off Weight

Maximum Landing Weight

Launched in: _____ Based on: _____
First Flight: _____ Entry Into Service: _____

——————— Basic Operation Data ———————

Engine Information: _____
_____

Transport Capacity: _____
_____

Range: _____
_____

——————— Aircraft Spotted ———————

Date/Time Spotted _____

Where/Location   _____

Airport Details   _____

_____

Notes

_____
_____
_____
_____

Aircraft Name_____

Aircraft Dimensions
Overall Length:

Height:

Fuselage Diameter:

Wingspan:

Wing Area:

Design Weight

Maximum Take Off Weight

Maximum Landing Weight

Launched in:_____ Based on:_____
First Flight: _____ Entry Into Service: _____

———— Basic Operation Data ————
Engine Information:_____
_____

Transport Capacity:_____
_____

Range:_____
_____

———— Aircraft Spotted ————
Date/Time Spotted_____

Where/Location   _____

Airport Details   _____

Notes
_____
_____
_____

Aircraft Name_____

Aircraft Dimensions
Overall **Length:**

Height:

Fuselage Diameter:

Wingspan:

Wing Area:

Design Weight

Maximum Take Off Weight

Maximum Landing Weight

Launched in:_____ Based on:_____
First Flight: _____ Entry Into Service: _____

———————Basic Operation Data———————

Engine Information:_____
_____

Transport Capacity:_____
_____

Range:_____
_____

——————— Aircraft Spotted ———————

Date/Time Spotted_____

Where/Location   _____

Airport Details   _____
_____

Notes
_____
_____
_____
_____

Aircraft Name _____

Aircraft Dimensions
Overall Length:

Height:

Fuselage Diameter:

Wingspan:

Wing Area:

Design Weight

Maximum Take Off Weight

Maximum Landing Weight

Launched in: _____ Based on: _____
First Flight: _____ Entry Into Service: _____

——————— Basic Operation Data ———————

Engine Information: _____

_____

Transport Capacity: _____

_____

Range: _____

_____

————— Aircraft Spotted —————

Date/Time Spotted _____

Where/Location _____

Airport Details _____

_____

Notes
_____
_____
_____
_____

Aircraft Name_____

Aircraft Dimensions
Overall Length:

Height:

Fuselage Diameter:

Wingspan:

Wing Area:

Design Weight

Maximum Take Off Weight

Maximum Landing Weight

Launched in:_____Based on:_____
First Flight: _____ Entry Into Service: _____

————Basic Operation Data————
Engine Information:_____
_____

Transport Capacity:_____
_____

Range: _____
_____

———— Aircraft Spotted ————
Date/Time Spotted_____

Where/Location   _____

Airport Details   _____

_____

Notes
_____
_____
_____
_____

Aircraft Name _____

Aircraft Dimensions
Overall Length:

Height:

Fuselage Diameter:

Wingspan:

Wing Area:

Design Weight

Maximum Take Off Weight

Maximum Landing Weight

Launched in: _____ Based on: _____
First Flight: _____ Entry Into Service: _____

———— Basic Operation Data ————

Engine Information: _____
_____

Transport Capacity: _____
_____

Range: _____
_____

———— Aircraft Spotted ————

Date/Time Spotted _____

Where/Location _____

Airport Details _____

_____

Notes
_____
_____
_____
_____

Aircraft Name _____

Aircraft Dimensions

Overall Length:

Height:

Fuselage Diameter:

Wingspan:

Wing Area:

Design Weight

Maximum Take Off Weight

Maximum Landing Weight

Launched in: _____ Based on: _____
First Flight: _____ Entry Into Service: _____

———— Basic Operation Data ————

Engine Information: _____
_____

Transport Capacity: _____
_____

Range: _____
_____

———— Aircraft Spotted ————

Date/Time Spotted _____

Where/Location   _____

Airport Details   _____
_____

Notes

_____
_____
_____
_____

Aircraft Name_____

Aircraft Dimensions

Overall Length:

Height:

Fuselage Diameter:

Wingspan:

Wing Area:

Design Weight

Maximum Take Off Weight

Maximum Landing Weight

Launched in:_____ Based on:_____
First Flight: _____ Entry Into Service: _____

———— Basic Operation Data ————

Engine Information:_____
_____

Transport Capacity:_____
_____

Range: _____
_____

———— Aircraft Spotted ————

Date/Time Spotted _____

Where/Location   _____

Airport Details _____

_____

Notes

_____
_____
_____
_____

Aircraft Name _____

Aircraft Dimensions
Overall **Length**:

Height:

Fuselage Diameter:

Wingspan:

Wing Area:

Design Weight

Maximum Take Off Weight

Maximum Landing Weight

Launched in: _____ Based on: _____
First Flight: _____ Entry Into Service: _____

——————— Basic Operation Data ———————
Engine Information: _____
_____

Transport Capacity: _____
_____

Range: _____
_____

——————— Aircraft Spotted ———————
Date/Time Spotted _____

Where/Location   _____

Airport Details   _____
_____

Notes
_____
_____
_____
_____

Aircraft Name _____

Aircraft Dimensions
Overall Length:

Height:

Fuselage Diameter:

Wingspan:

Wing Area:

Design Weight

Maximum Take Off Weight

Maximum Landing Weight

Launched in: _____ Based on: _____
First Flight: _____ Entry Into Service: _____

———— Basic Operation Data ————

Engine Information: _____

_____

Transport Capacity: _____

_____

Range: _____

_____

———— Aircraft Spotted ————

Date/Time Spotted _____

Where/Location   _____

Airport Details   _____

_____

Notes

_____
_____
_____
_____

Aircraft Name _____

Aircraft Dimensions
Overall **Length:**

Height:

Fuselage Diameter:

Wingspan:

Wing Area:

Design Weight

Maximum Take Off Weight

Maximum Landing Weight

Launched in:_____ Based on:_____
First Flight: _____ Entry Into Service: _____

——————Basic Operation Data——————
Engine Information:_____
_____

Transport Capacity:_____
_____

Range: _____
_____

—————— Aircraft Spotted ——————
Date/Time Spotted_____

Where/Location   _____

Airport Details   _____
_____

Notes
_____
_____
_____
_____

Aircraft Name_____

Aircraft Dimensions
Overall Length:

Height:

Fuselage Diameter:

Wingspan:

Wing Area:

Design Weight

Maximum Take Off Weight

Maximum Landing Weight

Launched in:_____ Based on:_____
First Flight: _____ Entry Into Service: _____

———— Basic Operation Data ————

Engine Information:_____
_____

Transport Capacity:_____
_____

Range: _____
_____

———— Aircraft Spotted ————

Date/Time Spotted _____

Where/Location   _____

Airport Details   _____

_____

Notes

_____
_____
_____
_____

Aircraft Name _____

Aircraft Dimensions

Overall **Length**:

Height:

Fuselage Diameter:

Wingspan:

Wing Area:

Design Weight

Maximum Take Off Weight

Maximum Landing Weight

Launched in: _____ Based on: _____
First Flight: _____ Entry Into Service: _____

——————— Basic Operation Data ———————

Engine Information: _____
_____

Transport Capacity: _____
_____

Range: _____
_____

——————— Aircraft Spotted ———————

Date/Time Spotted _____

Where/Location   _____

Airport Details   _____

_____

Notes

_____
_____
_____
_____

Aircraft Name _____

Aircraft Dimensions

Overall Length:

Height:

Fuselage Diameter:

Wingspan:

Wing Area:

Design Weight

Maximum Take Off Weight

Maximum Landing Weight

Launched in: _____ Based on: _____
First Flight: _____ Entry Into Service: _____

——————— Basic Operation Data ———————

Engine Information: _____
_____

Transport Capacity: _____
_____

Range: _____
_____

——————— Aircraft Spotted ———————

Date/Time Spotted _____

Where/Location   _____

Airport Details   _____

Notes
_____
_____
_____
_____

Aircraft Name _____

Aircraft Dimensions

Overall Length:

Height:

Fuselage Diameter:

Wingspan:

Wing Area:

Design Weight

Maximum Take Off Weight

Maximum Landing Weight

Launched in: _____ Based on: _____
First Flight: _____ Entry Into Service: _____

———— Basic Operation Data ————

Engine Information: _____
_____

Transport Capacity: _____
_____

Range: _____
_____

———— Aircraft Spotted ————

Date/Time Spotted _____

Where/Location _____

Airport Details _____
_____

Notes
_____
_____
_____
_____

Aircraft Name _____

Aircraft Dimensions

Overall Length:

Height:

Fuselage Diameter:

Wingspan:

Wing Area:

Design Weight

Maximum Take Off Weight

Maximum Landing Weight

Launched in:_____ Based on:_____
First Flight: _____ Entry Into Service: _____

———— Basic Operation Data ————

Engine Information:_____

_____

Transport Capacity:_____

_____

Range:_____

_____

———— Aircraft Spotted ————

Date/Time Spotted_____

Where/Location   _____

Airport Details   _____

Notes

_____
_____
_____
_____

Aircraft Name _____

Aircraft Dimensions
Overall **Length:**

Height:

Fuselage Diameter:

Wingspan:

Wing Area:

Design Weight

Maximum Take Off Weight

Maximum Landing Weight

Launched in: _____ Based on: _____
First Flight: _____ Entry Into Service: _____

———————Basic Operation Data———————

Engine Information: _____
_____

Transport Capacity: _____
_____

Range: _____
_____

——————— Aircraft Spotted ———————

Date/Time Spotted _____

Where/Location   _____

Airport Details   _____

Notes
_____
_____
_____
_____

Aircraft Name_____

Aircraft Dimensions

Overall Length:

Height:

Fuselage Diameter:

Wingspan:

Wing Area:

Design Weight

Maximum Take Off Weight

Maximum Landing Weight

Launched in:_____ Based on:_____
First Flight: _____ Entry Into Service: _____

———— Basic Operation Data ————

Engine Information:_____
_____

Transport Capacity:_____
_____

Range: _____
_____

———— Aircraft Spotted ————

Date/Time Spotted_____

Where/Location   _____

Airport Details   _____
_____

Notes
_____
_____
_____
_____

www.ingramcontent.com/pod-product-compliance
Lightning Source LLC
Chambersburg PA
CBHW071407080526
44587CB00017B/3198